SECRET LIVES OF
CAVE CREATURES

SECRET LIVES OF
CAVE CREATURES

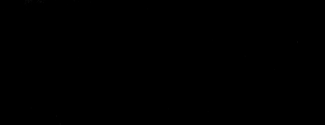

SARA SWAN MILLER

Marshall Cavendish
Benchmark
New York

The author and publisher would like to thank Sidney Horenstein, Geologist and Environmental Educator Emeritus, for his generous assistance in reading the manuscript.

EDITOR: JOYCE STANTON   PUBLISHER: MICHELLE BISSON
ART DIRECTOR: ANAHID HAMPARIAN   SERIES DESIGNER: KRISTEN BRANCH

Photo research by Laurie Platt Winfrey, Carousel Research
Cover: Photo Researchers, Inc:/ Dr. Merlin Tuttle, Bat Conservation International The photographs in this book are used by permission and through the courtesy of: *Animals/Animals:* David Dennis 29. © *Chip Clark: NSS, NMNH Smithsonian:* Titlepage,19, 20. 23, 29, 37. Corbis: Visuals Unlimited, 36. ©*William R. Elliott:* 39. © *Dante Fenolio/ www.anthoteca.com:* Half title, 11, 30, 33. *Getty Images:* Stephen Alvarez, National Geographic 8. *Jean Krejca/ Zara Environmental:* 16, 22 bottom. *National Geographic Images:* Rick Reid, 14; Stephen Alvarez, 40; Joel Sartore, 42. *Minden Pictures:* Kim Taylor 28. *Robert and Linda Mitchell:* Back Cover: *Photoshot:* NHPA, 41. *Visuals Unlimited:* William Johnson, 22 top; Garry Meszaros, 38; Dennis Kunkel/Microscopy, 42.

Printed in Malaysia (T)
135642

4666

Front cover: Bats are a common sight in caves.

Half-title page: A blind salamander walks on its skinny legs.

Title page: A cave salamander peeks out from a crevice in the rocks.

Back cover: This Texas blind salamander was found in Ezell's Cave near San Marcos, Texas.

CONTENTS

Visitors explore Mammoth Cave in Kentucky. About half a million people come to the enormous cave every year.

WHAT LIVES IN A ?

HAVE YOU EVER BEEN INSIDE A CAVE? If you have, did you see any animals there? Probably not. Cave creatures are very secretive. Most of them hide when strangers approach. A surprising number of animals, though, can be found in caves.

There are three different kinds of cave animals. Some just use the cave for temporary shelter. They are called trogloxenes (TRAH-glo-zeens), which means "cave guests." Other creatures spend most of their lives in the cave but also go outside to find food. These animals are called troglophiles (TRAH-glo-files), which means "cave lovers." Finally, there are the animals that are adapted to life in the dark caverns and cannot live anywhere else. This group is called troglobites (TRAH-glo-bites), which means "cave dwellers."

You can probably think of some trogloxenes. Raccoons sometimes find shelter in caves, and bears often spend winters inside, drowsing until spring comes. Skunks, pack rats, and some moths and beetles often take shelter in caves. Even some birds, such as cave swallows and phoebes, make their nests within the protection of a cave's rocky walls.

You are probably less familiar with troglophiles. They generally live farther inside than the trogloxenes. There are a number of these cave lovers. If you look carefully, you can spot some of them. Cave salamanders can be found climbing along the walls, enjoying the cave's cool, moist atmosphere.

Cave crickets lurk in the shadows, never uttering a sound. Cave spiders spin flat wheel-shaped webs in dark corners. Bats spend the day snoozing upside down in caves and come out at night to chase insects.

Deep in the darkest parts of the cave live the troglobites. These strange-looking creatures have evolved over thousands of years to become perfectly suited to cave life. They have lost the skin pigments that protect most creatures from the sun and have become either all white or pinkish in color.

This pale pink salamander lives deep within caves in Texas. The bright red feathery parts are its gills.

They cannot see. Because their habitat is dark, troglobites do not need the sense of sight. Instead of eyes, they rely on other well-developed sense organs to get around and find food. Blind flatworms, bristly cave crayfish, blind millipedes, blind salamanders, and cave springtails are among the many odd creatures known as troglobites.

What do cave creatures eat? There is hardly any food for herbivores, or plant eaters. Plants need sunlight to survive, so few can grow in caves. Some ferns and mosses can be found near a cave's entrance, but farther back there are only bacteria, molds, and fungi.

Still, there is a food chain in caves that supports the creatures that live inside. Decaying wood and leaves that wash into the cave provide food for tiny bacteria. Slightly larger, **aquatic** creatures, including small isopods, amphipods, and flatworms, eat the bacteria. Larger aquatic animals, such as salamanders,

REALLY BIG CAVES

Some caves are really enormous! The well-named Mammoth Cave in Kentucky has at least 365 miles (587 kilometers) of passageways. Imagine walking through the whole cave. If you walked at three miles an hour, it would take about 120 hours—five days and nights!

crayfish, and cave fish, live off these little creatures.

Bats, raccoons, bears, and other animals do their part by leaving droppings behind. Nonaquatic cave creatures, including snails, millipedes, beetles, and other insects, feed on the droppings and on the bodies of dead bats. These creatures, in turn, become food for spiders, crickets, and other animals.

A cave is home to more creatures than you would think. Hiding in its dark corners are all kinds of living things. Turn the page, and let's explore the secret lives of some of the most interesting cave creatures.

Swallow nests crowd
the entrance to a cave.

CAVE GUESTS

CAVE SWALLOWS

IN THE SPRING, cave swallows build their nests just inside the opening of a cave. They look for a perfect spot on the steep wall, then use their beaks to scoop up mud and bat **guano** from the cave floor. Beakful by beakful, they plaster the mud and droppings on the wall until, finally, they have made a cuplike nest. Then they swoop out of the cave to gather grass, fluffy bits of plants, and strands of bark to make a soft lining. Squeaking and twittering, they fly down to the ground and back to the nest, over and over again. Hundreds of cave swallows may build their nests in the same cave.

Each female lays three or four eggs in the finished nest. Once the eggs are laid, both parents take turns sitting on them. Finally, two weeks later, the hungry babies hatch. Now the hard work begins!

The parents spend the whole day hunting for flying insects to take to the hatchlings. They swoop through the air on their swift, pointed wings, snapping up flies, bugs,

RARE CAVE SWALLOWS
Cave swallows live only in parts of Texas, Arizona, and New Mexico.

beetles—even bees and wasps. Swallows do all their hunting on the wing. When they are thirsty, they swoop low over a stream and dip in their bills for a mouthful of water. Cave swallows hardly ever sit still, except at night, when they finally get to rest.

After about three weeks, the young have grown their feathers and are ready to leave the nest. They sit on the edge, flapping their wings to strengthen them. Then they swoop out of the cave to hunt their own insects.

PACK RATS

Pack rats are often cave guests. If you have ever watched one, you can easily guess how these creatures got their name. A pack rat likes to gather all kinds of strange things and bring them inside the cave to its nest. It likes shiny things best, including pieces of glass, coins, nails, and bits of aluminum foil. It also may collect feathers, pinecones, bits of rope, and cardboard. Sometimes a pack rat may be carrying a pinecone or feather and spot a shiny coin or piece of glass. It will simply drop what it is carrying and trade it for the shinier object. That's why pack rats are also called "trade rats."

Pack rats build their dome-shaped nests in a corner of a cave. They use sticks and leaves and decorate them with the odd objects they gather. Their houses keep them snug and help protect them from predators as they drowse through the daylight hours. Often, these nests are used over and over for a very long time. Some are thousands of years old!

At night, pack rats come out of the cave to forage for food. They like the leaves of shrubs and other plants, as well as fruits, seed heads, and pine needles. Sometimes they nibble on mushrooms and nuts. If they come across small insects, they will eat those, too.

Springtime is breeding time. Each male lives with two or three females and marks off his territory by spraying urine on the rocks. He will fight off any strange males that come around. A female gives birth to a litter of three to five babies.

A pack rat peeps out from its nest. It's probably a very old nest. Who knows how many other pack rats have lived in it?

In only about a month, the babies are ready to go off on their own. The mother soon has another litter and then another. That's a lot of baby pack rats coming into the world! But they have many enemies. Owls, coyotes, weasels, and bobcats all enjoy a tasty meal of pack rat.

Harvestmen, which look
a lot like spiders, can
also be found in caves.

CAVE LOVERS

CAVE SPIDERS

WHEN SUMMER COMES, a female cave spider spins a white silken holder for her eggs. Her egg case hangs by a thin thread from the ceiling inside the dark cave. The cave spider guards her precious eggs from any enemies that might come near. Other kinds of spiders may not live long enough to see their eggs hatch, but a cave spider can live for several years. Each year she will guard another egg case.

A spider's egg case can be huge.

A cave spider gets ready to devour its prey.

A cave spider is safe from most predators. It is covered with a sort of wax that is too hard for most other creatures to bite through. It also has very big jaws with sharp hooks that deliver quite a bite. When it bites, the cave spider shoots a powerful venom into its enemy.

Cave spiders spin flat wheel-shaped webs in the dim corners of the cave. Then they wait in ambush for an insect to get stuck in the sticky webbing. When a cave spider feels the vibrations of a struggling insect, it races over and bites its prey with its big jaws. Then it squirts its venom into the insect's body. The insect is quickly paralyzed, and the spider gobbles up its dinner.

Like most other spiders, cave spiders have eight eyes. But they have poor eyesight. They find their way about in the dim cave by using their sense of touch. Cave spiders are well adapted for cave life. They can be found in caves and cavelike places all over the world.

BATS

Of course you would expect to find bats in a cave. All winter long, they **hibernate**, hanging upside down from the ceiling. They nestle close together for warmth. When spring comes, they start to stir. They let out little squeaks as they slowly wake up.

Snuggling close, a colony of bats hang down from the ceiling of their cave.

Finally, at nightfall, first the females and then the males start streaming out of the cave, on the hunt for flying insects. The bats have not eaten all winter, and now they are ravenous. They soar over lakes, ponds, and marshes, where there are plenty of mosquitoes, flies, and other insects. As they fly, they let out beeps and squeaks to locate their prey. When a bat hears the echo of a beep bouncing off an insect, it starts beeping faster, homing in on its prey. It pops small insects right into its mouth. For larger ones, the bat folds its wing-to-tail membranes forward to make a pouch. In a flash, it scoops up the insect and flips its victim into its mouth. Then it flies on, hunting for more food.

FAST BEEPS

A bat may send out fourteen beeps in half a second to track its prey.

Little brown bats mate in the fall, but the females' eggs aren't fertilized right away. Instead, the females store the males' sperm in their bodies until springtime. After the

Baby leaf-nosed bats live together in the "nursery."

eggs are fertilized, the females leave their winter caves and move to a nesting spot in a different cave. They live together in big colonies. Females only! No males allowed! In the early summer, the babies are ready to be born.

When a mother bat gives birth, she switches her usual upside-down position and hangs from her thumbs. The baby bat comes out tail first, and the mother catches it in the same pouch she uses to scoop up insects. The baby climbs up its mother's body, latches onto a nipple, and begins to nurse.

For the first few days of the baby's life, it clings to its mother's belly as she flies about searching for insects. After that, the babies all stay together in one place while their mothers forage. By fall, the babies are big enough to fend for themselves. Then all the bats move back to their winter caves to hibernate.

CAVE CRICKETS

Cave crickets especially like **limestone** caves. There are usually more cave crickets than any other animal in a limestone cave. A big cave can be home to five thousand or more of them. But you might not even know they are there. These long-legged, spidery-looking crickets are well camouflaged. Their beige bodies blend in with the light brown limestone walls. You won't hear them chirping, either. Unlike most crickets, cave crickets are silent.

How do cave crickets find a mate without calling? They have very long **antennas**, which can sense vibrations and

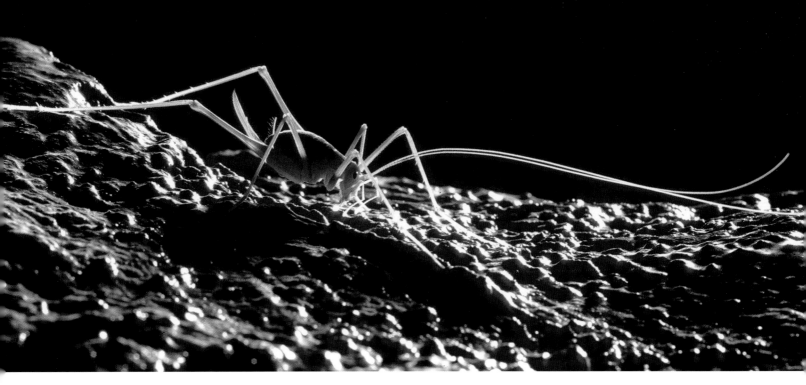

guide them to a partner. After a female mates in the summer, she lays her eggs one by one in the loose soil. With her long **ovipositor**, she can lay them deep in the dirt. The eggs rest there all winter. They won't hatch until late spring.

Cave crickets are hard to spot in the dark.

Cave crickets also use their antennas to find their way around in the dark cave. At night, they may come out of the cave to feed, finding their food mostly by feel. They eat all

OTHER PLACES TO LIVE

Cave crickets live in other places besides caves, including wells, hollow logs, and even damp basements.

kinds of things—leaf bits, fruit, roots, fungus, dead insects, even dead cave crickets.

Because they go in and out of the cave, cave crickets help support other life there. They bring in fungus spores, which later sprout, and they leave their droppings all over the cave floor. Smaller creatures that live inside the cave all their lives feed on the fungus and on the droppings. Without cave crickets, there would be many fewer creatures living inside a cave.

Cave Salamanders

Cave salamanders are very common cave lovers. You might see one hanging from the cave wall with its long **prehensile**

More Homes for Salamanders

Like cave crickets, cave salamanders like damp basements as well as caves.

tail. Watch, and you may see the salamander spot a fly zipping by. In a flash, it lunges at the fly, shooting out its long tongue. *Gulp!* The fly vanishes down the salamander's throat.

Cave salamanders spend most of their time clambering around the walls of the cave, searching for insects, slugs, worms, and other **invertebrate** prey. Sometimes they go out in the woods to forage under rocks and logs.

Most cave salamanders have no lungs. How do they breathe? As long as their skin stays moist, they can take in oxygen through their skin pores. Damp caves and cave streams are the perfect home for cave salamanders.

This kind of cave salamander lives only in the Midwest and in some southern states.

This isopod only looks big. It is actually less than a quarter of an inch (6 millimeters) long.

CAVE DWELLERS

CAVE ISOPODS

HAVE YOU EVER heard of isopods? Hundreds of **species** of isopods live all over the world, but they are so small that you may never have noticed them. They all breathe with gills, so they need to live in the water or in damp places like caves.

An isopod may remind you of a tiny shrimp. But there is a way of telling an isopod apart from other **crustaceans.**

Extending from the end of its abdomen is a single pair of leaflike parts called uropods. Other crustaceans have several pairs of uropods. An isopod can use its uropods to help it swim. It also gets around, on both land and water, with its seven pairs of legs, which are attached to the seven segments of its **thorax**.

The Madison cave isopod, which lives far inside a cave, is blind. How does it find food and mates? It uses its two pairs of antennas. The first pair senses food chemicals, and the second pair feels vibrations that lead the isopod to a mate.

At mating time, a female climbs onto a male's back, and he carts her around for a while. After they mate, the female carries her eggs in pouches on her belly. When the babies hatch, they look like

ISOPODS IN DANGER

Many species of cave isopods, including the Madison cave isopod, are now threatened, mostly because of pollution seeping into the caves. This worries scientists because many other cave creatures feed on isopods. Without the isopods, other cave creatures would soon die off. Isopods may be tiny, but they are hugely important.

miniature adults. Off they go to scavenge for bits of decaying plants and bat droppings.

CAVE AMPHIPODS

Cave amphipods are only a little bigger than isopods. They look a lot like isopods, too, except that they have three pairs of uropods instead of just one. They live in the cold waters deep inside a cave, feeding on tiny dead plants and animals. In turn, fish, salamanders, and crayfish feed on the amphipods. Amphipods, like isopods, are an important link in the food chain.

A cave amphipod looks much like an isopod. Both are important links in the food chain.

There are more than seven thousand kinds of amphipods living all around the world. Some live in oceans, some in marshes, and some in wet places on land. Although that number sounds like a lot, amphipods are in danger. For example, Illinois cave amphipods used to live in six cave systems in that state. Now scientists are finding them in only three. The U.S. Fish and Wildlife Service has put them on its list of endangered species.

What is happening to the cave amphipods? The waters in their caves have become polluted. When farmers use pesticides and fertilizers on their crops, they pollute the groundwater that seeps into the caves. Human sewage, cow droppings, and even toxic wastes also find their way into the waters that feed the caves. Cave

BAD NEWS FOR PEOPLE, TOO

The shrinking population of Illinois cave amphipods is a bad sign, not just for the health of the caves, but for people living in the area. The disappearance of the amphipods is like a red flag, warning people that their drinking water may be polluted, too.

amphipods are very sensitive to these pollutants and are in danger of being lost forever.

BLIND FLATWORMS

Another cave dweller is the blind flatworm. Blind flatworms are totally blind, but they still manage to move about and find food. They live in dark streams deep inside caves, where there isn't enough light to see anything. They have sense organs that detect chemicals in the water so they can tell when food is nearby. They also have balance sensors that keep them on an even keel and other sensors that detect water movement.

Flatworms wriggle through the water by flexing their muscles. On land, they can lay down a trail of slime and move along by beating their cilia. These tiny hairlike parts beat constantly. For food, flatworms

LOOKING FOR FLATWORMS?

Blind flatworms are hard to see because they are so small. They are only one-fifth of an inch (5 millimeters) long.

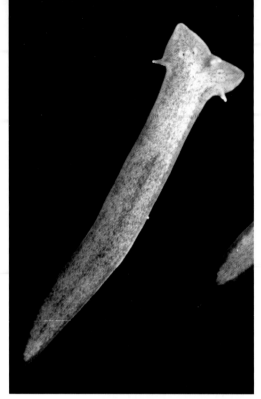

This flatworm has grown two heads from one that was cut.

eat other tiny organisms, such as isopods, or graze on bat guano that has dropped to the floor of the cave.

Flatworms are very simple animals. They don't even have a stomach. The food passes down their throat and gets absorbed by cells in the empty spaces inside. They don't have a respiratory system or a circulatory system, either. They absorb oxygen and fluids through their skin.

An amazing thing about cave-dwelling flatworms is that they can regrow parts of their bodies. If a flatworm's head is cut in half, it will grow two heads from the halves. Some flatworms can grow a whole new body from just a tiny piece.

Until they reach a certain length, flatworms reproduce by mating with other flatworms. When they get bigger, they don't need to mate. Instead, the rear parts of their bodies split off and grow into new flatworms.

SECRET LIVES OF CAVE CREATURES

BRISTLY CAVE CRAYFISH

Bristly cave crayfish also live all their lives in caves. It's not hard to guess how this freshwater crustacean, which looks like a small all-white lobster, got its name. On its long, narrow pincers are many bristles, or short stiff hairs. Since it is almost completely blind, the crayfish needs these bristles to feel its way around in the dark. It does have tiny eyes, but they can only make out light and dark.

The bristly cave crayfish has very long antennas compared to other species of crayfish. On the antennas are sensory cells that help the crayfish detect chemicals in the water and find

Cave crayfish may live more than one hundred years.

BERRY GOOD!

A female crayfish is a good mother. Her hundreds of eggs are attached to her swimmerets, which protect them from predators as she carries them around. An egg-laying female is said to be "in berry," because her mass of eggs looks like a raspberry.

food and mates. Its favorite foods are isopods, amphipods, insect **larvae**, and flatworms. On its four pairs of walking legs, the crayfish crawls along the bottom of a stream. It uses the five pairs of swimmerets on its abdomen to help it move. When a crayfish finds food, it grabs its prey with its strong claws. Usually, crayfish creep along slowly, but if one is startled, it will flip its tail rapidly and shoot back to safety.

BLIND MILLIPEDES

There are plenty of blind millipedes deep in a cave, too. Some kinds of millipedes can grow up to nearly a foot long, but blind millipedes are tiny—never more than an inch and

a half. These all-white millipedes hide in the soil or in bits of leaf litter on the cave floor. Even if you have a powerful flashlight, they are hard to spot.

Even though they can't see, blind millipedes can move quickly.

Millipedes need to live in damp places, so a cave is the perfect spot for them. Like insects, millipedes breathe through tubes along their bodies, called spiracles. But, unlike insects, they can't close up their spiracles. Because of that, they can dry out easily. They also have a problem if they fall into the water. They can't keep the water out of their spiracles and can quickly drown.

A LOT OF LEGS

Millipede means "thousand-legs." Even though they look as if they might have that many legs, most millipedes have no more than three hundred—two pairs on each body segment. Still, that's a lot of legs to coordinate!

There isn't much for blind millipedes to eat deep in a cave. Mostly, they feed on bacteria and fungi. They have simple chewing mouths with taste buds along the sides.

All millipedes move their legs in waves to push themselves along and burrow into the soil. Most species move slowly. Blind millipedes, though, are faster than others. They can even climb up the cave walls, gripping with the little claws on the ends of their legs.

At mating time, a male millipede walks along a female's back to attract her attention. After mating, the female makes a nest of her droppings and lays a few hundred eggs. After they hatch, the babies stay inside the nest for a few days, growing and **molting** several times before they are ready to go off on their own.

This spring-tail is extremely small—only 1/16th of an inch (1.5 millimeters) long.

CAVE SPRINGTAILS

What are those tiny insects hopping around on the cave floor? Are they fleas? They hop like fleas, but take a closer look and you can tell the difference. Fleas are dark and flattened, but cave springtails are pale and rounded. Cave springtails are also furry, not bald like fleas. Their species name, *hirsuta*, means "hairy."

Fleas leap by flexing their long legs, but springtails have a completely different way of hopping. Under their abdomen is an organ called a furcula. Usually, the furcula is folded up and held by a kind of catch. But when a springtail is alarmed, it triggers its furcula, which catapults it into the air. A springtail will

GREAT LEAPERS

A springtail can jump fifteen times its length!

keep on catapulting itself until it finds a safe place to hide.

Like other springtails, cave springtails prefer cool, damp places under stones. Using their short legs, they run under and around soil particles on the cave floor. They find plenty of things to eat with their tiny chewing mouths. Bits of algae, bacteria, fungi, and rotting plant matter are all food for a springtail. On the underside of its abdomen, a springtail has a little tube called a collophore. The springtail uses its collophore to suck up water.

In the spring, female springtails make tiny holes in the soil and scatter their eggs in them. When they hatch, the babies look like adults, only they are extremely small. These **nymphs** feed hungrily all summer. By winter, they are fully grown and springing about on the cave floor like their parents.

TEXAS BLIND SALAMANDERS

The strange-looking Texas blind salamander lives only in caves in Hays County, Texas. Unlike some other cave salamanders, it spends all of its time in caves. It looks pink because its skin is **translucent** and you can see its blood vessels showing through. You can even see its internal organs! Its skinny legs are like little toothpicks. It rarely needs to walk, anyway, because it stays in the water all its life. It uses its finned tail to swim about.

Texas blind salamanders are very rare.

BREEDING ANYTIME

There are no seasons in a cave, so cave salamanders can breed all year long.

Most salamanders, when they are larvae, have gills in order to breathe. As they grow into adults, they lose their gills and breathe with their lungs or through their skin. But Texas blind salamanders never lose their bright red gills. Since they never leave the water, lungs would do them no good at all.

Because it cannot see, the Texas blind salamander finds its food by smell and touch. It feeds on isopods, amphipods, snails, shrimps, and other small creatures in the dark cave streams.

When a female is ready to mate, it's her job to get a male interested. First, she rubs her chin along his back. If that doesn't work, she scratches at him and fans her tail at him. Then, if he keeps on ignoring her, she may nip at his sides. That usually works!

The Texas blind salamander is only one of the many unusual creatures that live in our caves. If we work to protect our environment and keep our caves free from pollution, we can keep it—and all the other cave creatures—around for a long, long time.

Words to Know

antennas The long, thin body parts on the heads of some creatures, such as insects, that are used to sense touch or smell. Antennas come in pairs.

aquatic Living in the water.

crustacean A class of mostly aquatic animals with an outer skeleton and a pair of legs on each body segment.

guano A name for the droppings of some animals, such as bats and birds.

hibernate To spend the winter in a deep sleep.

invertebrate An animal without a backbone.

larvae The young of many invertebrates.

limestone A soft stone made up mostly of the mineral calcite.

molting Shedding skin, fur, or feathers periodically.

nymphs The young of some animals, such as some insects.

ovipositor A tube at the end of a female invertebrate's abdomen, used for laying eggs.

prehensile Able to grip, such as a tail.

species A group of animals or plants that have many characteristics in common. Members of the same species can mate and bear offspring.

thorax The middle part of some animals.

translucent Capable of letting light through.

U.S. Fish and Wildlife Service A government organization that works to protect wildlife.

Learning More

BOOKS

Aulenbach, Nancy Holler, Hazel A. Barton, and Marfé Ferguson Delano. *Exploring Caves: Journeys into the Earth.* Washington, DC: National Geographic, 2001.

Brimner, Larry Dane. *Caves.* Danbury, CT: Children's Press, 2000.

Gallant, Roy A. *Limestone Caves.* Danbury, CT: Franklin Watts, 1998.

Taylor, Michael Ray. *Caves: Exploring Hidden Realms.* Washington, DC: National Geographic, 2001.

VIDEOS AND DVDS

Journey in Amazing Caves. Image Entertainment, 2001.

Mammoth Cave National Park, Kentucky. Finley Holiday Film Corp., 2002.

Nova: Mysterious Life of Caves. WGBH Studio, 2008.

INTERNET SITES

Amazing Bats of Bracken Cave

http://kids.nationalgeographic.com/Stories/AnimalsNature/Bat-cave
Find out about the 20 million bats (and assorted insects) that live in Bracken Cave in Texas.

Kid's Cave

www.cavern.org/acca/kidscave.php
The American Cave Conservation Association offers fun activities for

young cave explorers, including puzzles, riddles, coloring pages, and instructions for building a bat house.

National Caves Association

http://cavern.com

This site contains a directory of caves, facts about caves and what lives in them, and a spotlight on particular caves and caverns.

Index

Page numbers for illustrations are in boldface

About the Author

SARA SWAN MILLER has written more than sixty books for young people. She has enjoyed working with children all her life, first as a Montessori nursery-school teacher and later as an outdoor environmental educator at the Mohonk Preserve in New Paltz, New York. The best part of her work is helping kids appreciate the beauty of the natural world.